HOKKAIDO JOURNAL

Ten days hitchhiking in northern Japan
June 1-10, 1973

Ellie Caldwell

Production Editor: Gary Caldwell
Map: Thecla Geraghty
Cover art: Dreamstime, Natalia Darmoroz

Caldwell, Ellie,
HOKKAIDO JOURNAL
1. Travel 2. Japan 3. Feminism

Published in paperback and as an eBook by Amazon
and Amazon Kindle.

DEDICATION:
To those who have a yen for seeing the world.

Also by Ellie Caldwell

Available from Southeastern Yearly Meeting:
The Little Quaker Book of De-Clutter

Available from Amazon, print and eBook:
*The Little Quaker Book of Time Mis-Management:
    How Wasting Time Is Good for the Soul*
*Your God is Just Wrong: A Continuation of
    Revelation*
This Way In: The Inner Life
Being Church in An Unchurched World
It's Not About Us: The Complications of Caregiving
Give Way: A Lifetime of Surrender
*Through the Eyes of Another: Continuing the
    Conversation on Race*
The 21st Century Pandemic: Grief and Gifts

Available as eBooks from Amazon Kindle:
*We Don't Have to Get Sick (To Get the Attention We
    Need)*
The Little Quaker Book of Weight Loss
The Little Quaker Book of De-Clutter
*Why Our Kids Hate Us (And How They Probably
    Really Don't)*
*Rising Still: Breaking Through the Sadness of
    Women*
*Knock, Knock, Who's There? Being Real in an Unreal
    World & Vice Versa*
How to (Somewhat) Disaster-Proof Your Life

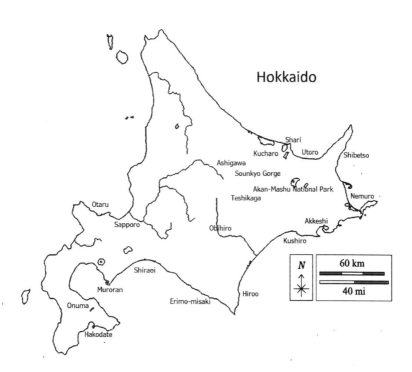

INTRODUCTION

May I introduce you to *Hokkaido Journal,* the notebook I kept June 1-10, 1973, as I hitchhiked around Hokkaido, the northernmost large island of Japan.

I hadn't expected to hitchhike, planned to take buses and stay at youth hostels, but soon found I "couldn't get there from here" so stuck out my thumb.

By that time, I'd been in Japan for two years. How I got there is a long story. The entire tale isn't necessary, but a brief version will place these ten days in context.

It started with a little girl growing up in southern Maine reading a lot and dreaming of adventures. Robert Louis Stevenson's "The Sun's Travels" in *A Child's Garden of Verses,* caught my attention: the sun and moon appearing at opposite times to Asian children and me.

I went off to the University of New Hampshire (UNH), but after three years, dropped out and spent a year in Denver with Volunteers in Service to America (VISTA). Living in public housing and working on community programs, I met people whose first language wasn't English, an eye-opener. My life took a liberal turn and never went back.

I returned to UNH to live in an off-campus apartment with three other students and finish my senior year. The day before graduation, I found I had four credits left to graduate. (What you get for depending on your adviser to keep track!) With my mother and sister coming for graduation, I walked in the procession but received an empty diploma folder. (A year later, I submitted a paper on daycare in San Francisco to a professor I'd babysat for, got a B and a degree.)

I found a three-credit film course and stayed on in the apartment through the summer. We gave some great parties,

1

including one for the first moon landing. Semester over, I left in a VW van with a couple of friends for San Francisco, the mecca of the day.

For the next year, I lived in a couple of communes, hung around Golden Gate Park, worked temp jobs, and lived The 60s. I look back now, remember the Vietnam War and the protests, but realize how little the war affected me. Also, despite the love and peace, there was extensive negativity: e.g., drug use, sexism, and police violence.

During the year, I got involved with a guy named Craig (not real name) whose ex-girlfriend's brother had taught at *Nichibei Gakuin* (Japan-American Academy) in Kochi, a small city on the island of Shikoku, Japan, that was always looking for English teachers. Craig could talk of nothing else and within a year, had his ticket. He and others used to say there was going to be a revolution soon and if we didn't want to pick up weapons, we'd better leave the country.

Before he left, I'd gone back to Maine to visit my family. At some point, Craig showed up, looking like husband-to-be material (in my mother's eyes), and calming everyone down. Not the shaggy-haired hippie they expected.

He went off to Japan, and I got a job as a teacher's aide at an elementary school in a nearby town. I moved into an apartment near the school and spent the year writing letters and planning to join him in a year.

In 1971, diplomatic wrangling between Japan and the US, called the Nixon *shocku,* slowed the visa process. Waiting in San Francisco, I stayed with friends and spent time at a library in Japantown researching the status of women in Japan

I arrived in Japan with $200 and no return ticket. The school was supposed to guarantee travel to and from Japan, but we somehow knew not to expect it.

Craig was living in a seaside villa that someone had loaned him. The school rented me a small backyard three-room house owned by a widow named Mrs. Tanaka, a luxury for the average Japanese. With a Western toilet! The first night, returning after dark, I couldn't find the house, wandered around by streetlight, and was rescued by two young women out walking. I've had many nightmares like this over the years! Traveling has its stresses!

The main room had lovely *tatami* mat floors and a *kotatsu,* a low table with heater under it and covered by a quilt. Cozy during the chilly winter!

Midyear, I was adopted by a calico cat we named "Henna Gaijin" (Strange Foreigner). I was used to living with cats and enjoyed the company.

However, the Japanese view of cats then wasn't particularly benign, and some people feared them. One day I found him dead on my steps, probably poisoned.

I didn't want to ask for a shovel to bury him in Mrs. Tanaka's back yard (and didn't have the Japanese). So I found a large box, put him in, sealed the box well, and took the bus to Craig's villa. With ceremony, Henna Gaijin was buried in the backyard by the sea

The language school was the first time I'd ever taught. The head of the school opened the classroom door and shoved me in. I bowed properly, sat down, introduced myself, and asked for questions.

Right away, someone asked, "Are you and Mr. S 'rubbers'?" As I was still adjusting to Japanese-accented English, it took a moment to realize he was asking if we were "lovers." I replied stiffly that we were friends.

Gradually I adapted to the classroom schedule and expectations. Students were attentive and well-behaved, spoiling me for American college freshmen later.

One memorable class happened with a group of elementary students I was struggling with: "What is this? Is this a cup? No, it is not a cup. It is a pen."

The class repeated my words mechanically, then suddenly one boy got it, and the room exploded! "Is this a cup?!" "Yes, it is a cup!" Loud and total chaos for the rest of the class. Delightful!

Those notes from the Japanese library in SF and my copy of *Our Bodies Ourselves* later became the basis of a conversation class with older teenage girls, part of their last—and only—time of freedom between high school and marriage.

They were learning *koto* (Japanese zither), needlework, housekeeping, and English to prepare to be Japanese housewives. In the class, we exchanged information about Japanese and US laws related to women, and I shared *OBO* chapters on women's health and birth control. It was one of my most satisfying teaching experiences; we all learned a lot.

After a year, Craig decided to move to Kyoto. For the next few months, I took a late afternoon train up the coast of Shikoku on Friday, then a ferry, and another train, learning to sleep on all of them, and arrived at his *gasshuku* (student rooming house) around 8am Saturday. On Sunday afternoon, I'd repeat the trip and be in class by 8am Monday. Once, there was a landslide on the track up ahead and another time a blackout so we sat in the dark for a couple hours.

After a few months, I moved into his *gasshuku in* Kyoto and taught at different private companies. These jobs just seemed to come to us; the *gaijin* grapevine, I suppose. At *Mitsubishi Denki* (Electric), I had the pleasure of witnessing the employees rise to their feet every morning to robustly sing the company song with fervor, a morning ritual in many Japanese companies.

Inside temple grounds, the *gasshuku* was on the side of a mountain outside downtown Kyoto. For weeks we heard a high-pitched whistle early in the morning, like the loons in New Hampshire. It turned out to be the local tofu truck. I got in the habit of taking a basin down and joining the other women in

4

line to buy fresh tofu. Also a vegetable truck came up occasionally.

The *gasshuku* was typical student housing with a half a dozen other young people. We didn't interact much but got to know them in the shared kitchen as they made their ramen. The *benjo* (toilet) was an old-fashioned hole in the floor that one perched perilously above. I lost a bedroom slipper down there once; not the first time it's happened, I'm sure.

The *gasshuku* had an outside sink area where we washed up, but no bath so we sometimes walked down to the public bath. I washed our clothes at the outside sink, including sheets. It got chilly in the winter and sometimes they'd freeze on the line.

We had two rather large *tatami* mat rooms. Mine had an improvised desk along one wall where I spent a lot of time writing. We had a small dorm-style refrigerator. I look back now and it seems very primitive but the setting was beautiful with maples and irises.

Years later, I met an American from New York who'd stayed in the same *gasshuku* five years after us. Small world, but Chris said casually, "Oh, not so unusual. A popular *gaijin* spot after all."

On New Year's Day, we were expected to visit the woman who oversaw the temple grounds. I knelt in the doorway, bowed deeply, and repeated New Year's greetings in Japanese.

One amazing fact of living in the *gasshuku* was how cheap life was. I could support myself working nine hours a week, and we even had government health insurance.

I look back at my 20s and know my own children haven't been able to explore as freely; adventure is much more expensive now.

Through some of the Westerners living in Kyoto, we got an entry to the Zen training given for *gaijins* by Kobori Roshi

(Teacher Kabori) at Daitokuji Temple. Craig went for a while and then I decided to join him.

In the interview, I was not presenting myself as a particularly spiritual soul. (The idea of ten minutes of meditation freaked me out!) But when the Roshi hesitated, I teared up, and he let me in. (I remember thinking, "Gosh, tears work on Zen priests too." Craven American woman.)

The temple was an introduction to meditation, still with me today, but also to Zen Buddhism. We sat on an L-shaped ledge, some in full- or half-lotus and others perched on a *zabuton* cushion. (I left Japan with calluses on both ankles from sitting on my heels on *tatami.*)

Occasionally we had *dokusan* (private sessions) with the Sensei. One time I requested the traditional *kyosaku or* "wake up" stick for encouragement. The novice hit me on one shoulder and then the other. It just felt like punishment to me; some things don't translate well. In addition, we sometimes had walking in the courtyard, a peaceful way to meditate.

One time the Sensei broke the silence with "*Oto daru na!*" that shook the room. I never knew what it meant, but years later, a Lutheran missionary translated it: "Be quiet!" We could be fidgety!

Once we participated in a traditional Japanese tea ceremony, which necessitated a lot of graceful movements across the *tatami* floor by an American woman in a kimono following the strict procedures. The Sensei said, "Look, she's almost as good as a Japanese woman," which made me inwardly curl my lip.

The other students were mostly men and quite pleased with themselves. I wasn't having much of it. I'd get back to the *gasshuku*, have a beer, and probably spill it on the *tatami.*

By then our relationship had crumbled, and Craig was spending many hours hanging out with friends at bars in

6

Kyoto. Occasionally he'd come back at 11pm and I would get out of bed and prepare tea and snacks for him and his friends.

At the time that felt acceptable as well as hand washing clothes in freezing water, but it took its toll. I came out of those two years feeling diminished and low spirited.

One highlight was meeting an Australian woman, Sandra Sewell, at the train station in Osaka. We started talking, decided to get coffee and cakes, and spent the next four hours talking. (I think she says five hours.)

We've continued to be friends for the last 50 years. We used to send blue aerograms back and forth and now email. She visited me in Boston and Florida, and I visited her in Canada and twice on Tamborine Mountain outside Brisbane, Australia.

When visas ran out, foreign residents went to South Korea and re-entered the country. Craig decided he'd travel through Europe and back through the US. After he left, I finished up my teaching jobs and decided to plan a farewell trip on my own.

Other Western women got jobs in bars as hostesses. Similar to barmaids around the world, they flirted, sat on laps, enticed men to drink, and got big tips. Two of them took over our rooms at the *gasshuku.* Their chilling stories made me glad I'd been able to find teaching jobs.

One good part of knowing Craig was his enthusiasm to see Japan. We'd had day excursions to various parks, temples, and nearby cities around Kyoto. In 1972, I took the train on my own to Kobe to the American Embassy to vote for George McGovern. Another time, I traveled with a young Swiss woman and her Japanese boyfriend to the island of Kyushu. I loved leaving the house every morning knowing I might see something I'd never seen in my life.

After two years, as I planned my departure from Japan, I thought about the one area I'd always wanted to see:

Hokkaido. It was lovely in pictures, like New England, less populated, and had a rich history of the Indigenous Ainu people. I wasn't overly confident in my Japanese but figured I could manage, find youth hostels, and meet young people who wanted to practice English. So off I went.

I took a notebook along to jot down thoughts and later realized its importance for mental balance after whole days immersed in Japanese. It's been sitting in my desk for a number of years and now feels like the time to share this adventure. I suppose it's part of the wrapping up we do towards the end of our lives, but also somewhat a nostalgic return to a more adventurous time.

I should add that there has been minimal editing, mostly to take handwritten pages written for oneself into a form accessible to others. That has meant changing tenses and clarifying the Japanese. I've debated and discussed with others how to make the translations work—from slashes to footnotes to an end page—and have decided I like the immediate, on-the-line reference and have tried not to assume a reader would pick up terms quickly. I'd been there two years and that's how we talked, throwing in occasional Japanese words or phrases that said something better than we could say in English, part of how we were becoming familiar with the culture.

A friend said, "It must be fun to read your own words from 50 years ago and see the seeds of who you've become." Wise words!

What do I see when I read the words of Ellie Mitchell? At first it feels embarrassing: Naïve, politically-minded, but steeped in the culture she'd grown up in. A young woman inevitably affected by a relationship with a man and the world around her, but also determined to be optimistic and open to new experiences.

The Ugly American had come out in 1958 and Americans like me were determined to show another side. In fact, I see I was prepared to burn out my eyeballs and get headaches not wearing sunglasses, and I suspect I didn't have a sunhat or sunscreen either. Image is everything! Until it isn't!

I recognize how rough those two years were in some ways, but I also applaud her adventurous spirit and willingness to welcome new experiences, although maybe not a raw egg at breakfast.

Our lives are made up of so many "selves": Two-year-old brat, noisy five-year-old, sullen teenager, serious student, daughter, employee, traveler. We're all of that, and by the time we reach our 70s, we're well-seasoned. Our seasons show us who we've been, how we became who we are now, and how we've lived out the dreams of our youth.

I hope you enjoy reading about this short period of my life, and perhaps it will inspire you to look at your past. One of the gifts we can give our children and grandchildren is a sense of how we became the people we are.

Okay, they may not be dying to hear stories of grandma's wild hippie past and maybe you don't have grandchildren, but memories can frame our lives. As we age, it becomes important to extract meaning from our history and understand why we've been here.

Write it for family, for friends, but also, for yourself. Our lives are precious gifts we've received, but also precious as gifts we give ourselves and others.

Before I close, I'd like to put in a plug for living abroad when we're young. We learn the value of other cultures, meet "the foreigner" face to face, and see ourselves as someone else's "other." We broaden our ideas of what it's like for others to live their daily lives, work, raise children, and have hopes and dreams.

9

People think it's hard to work abroad now, more expensive and not as safe as in the past. I'd agree to some extent and should also add that I would not recommend repeating my stunt. My 10 days hitchhiking in Hokkaido could have had an entirely different ending; there was some luck involved.

But there are still many opportunities for travel for those interested in living abroad. For instance, any English speaker with a college degree can teach at a school in South Korea.

Everywhere in the world there are service jobs in restaurants or hotels. Or teaching jobs on military bases, which I hear are the best teaching jobs in the world. American Embassies are a good source for information. I've also met people who traveled as nannies, nurses, or pet sitters, getting to see the world while making money.

We need to get out of our own bubbles, learn to function in other cultures and languages, and come home better able to participate in our multicultural world. It takes a village, they say, to raise kids, but also to make a community, care for each other, deal with social problems, and create a loving and peaceful world.

Gambatte! Go for it!

My favorite thing to do is to go where I've never been.
Diane Arbus

HOKKAIDO JOURNAL

June 1, 1973, Friday. Aboard the Honshu-Hokkaido Ferry.

I have been well looked out for so far, reassuring when one knows so little about what's going on.

I nearly missed the train out of Kyoto in the first place. After many wrong directions, I finally found a kind conductor who took five minutes to explain the intricate routes of the train which happened to be leaving in seven minutes.

Once I got to Tsuruga for the ferry, a helpful guard walked me all the way to the bus stop, complimented my hobbling Japanese, and gave the driver strict instructions for my welfare. (At least I think that's what he was saying).

I got off at the right stop and walked ten minutes to the ferry amid rows of construction workers yelling, "*Herro, herro!*" (Hello! Hello!) and "Hitchhike *suru*?" ("Do you hitchhike?") Then to the ferry office where someone helped with filling out the forms. And then upstairs to wait for the ferry to board.

We waited. Five million strong it seemed, packed *ippai* (to the gills). We waited. And waited. Then, very, very slowly we began to board the ark, one group after another, two by two of all the specimens available.

A young clerk at the door let me know over all the heads when it was my turn to board. At times like this, when one is swept up among so many faces, there is a large gratitude that many people here are very kind. Also that I'm tall.

Apparently I'm the only *gaijin* (foreigner) aboard this enormous tub, but there are so many people, one would never know. There must be as many people aboard as in my hometown in Maine. Herds, packs, squads of them! And a good number are the typical *gaijin* starers that abounded in Kochi last year.

The young males are troublesome when drunk, but generally tolerable. Seems like there might be a few young people I'll be able to talk with. Pleasant young women with babies, young hip kids with their *kakkui* (groovy) denim overalls. Rather *okashi* (funny).

I was assigned a Special Second Class room for five. (I was glad it was Special and not the regular Second Class, large corral-like areas lined off in carpeted squares.) I shared this room with four faintly dubious Japanese males, magazine readers, mah jongg players, and, undoubtedly, beer drinkers. Later corrections: They played *shogi* (Japanese chess) and drank *sake*, not beer. Probably they were slightly higher level office workers than I thought. But maybe not.

I returned from lunch in the dining room and a turn about the upper deck, but still no sign of the ferry leaving. As I sat down to write, *Auld Lang Syne* came blaring through the loudspeaker, a definite sign in Japan of departure. I went out with the others to the deck as the ship began to shudder in anticipation. (Or was it just all those bodies moving starboard?)

Red, yellow, and blue streamers stretched from deck to shore, colorfully waving in the breeze. All the ferry employees were out on the dock, along with people seeing passengers off. I tried to avoid the crowd and strolled casually around the deck to the once traditional-Scottish, now traditional-Japanese, melody.

Then I went down and stood with the others, watching as the office clerks tossed up the ropes. As the ferry began to move in earnest, everyone waved back and forth, laughing and calling out to friends on shore.

Even the employees managed to look enthusiastic, although it must have been a daily event for them.

"Goodbye! Have a good trip! Farewell! Bye, bye! Sayonara! Bye, bye!" All I could think was, "God, how corny, how syrupy, sentimental, yuck!"

But in the middle of all those blank, practiced faces on shore, I caught the tragic face of an old *ojisan* (grandfather) who looked as if everything beautiful in his life was leaving on the ferry. At once, tears came to my eyes.

Farewells are so sad. Goodbye, a fast kiss, and there you are. Left behind. I stood at the rail with the other passengers, tears falling down my face, even though it was my vacation and I wasn't leaving anyone at all.

My dear, do please watch these emotional outbursts! How will you ever say goodbye when you do leave Japan in a couple of months? Maybe if you get through all these vicarious departures, the impact of the real one will lessen.

There was something so beautiful in that old man's face: exhilarating, tragic, and joyful simultaneously. Life is incredibly sad at such moments, with one's grandchildren floating away on the ferry, but in spite of it—because of it—there is still joy, laughter, and tomorrow too.

Human beings are fine creatures, at least as seen from ship decks. Going by water is also certainly fine, romantic, and very "there." Ancient and strong.

So we five in "Special Second Class" made acquaintances and asked all the askable questions, plus a few others. One rather boorish fellow must have thought I was making a Hokkaido money plan while I wrote; he asked how much it was going to cost. Not quite as rude as I thought he was.

My other roommates are all pleasant 30+ year-old workers from Kobe on a holiday, with all the predictable thoughts on the state of Japanese and American life and quite a lot of unpredictable kindness. With the exception of that one boor asking all sorts of questions about why I wasn't married. That's rude in any language, Japanese or English.

We waited endlessly for dinner until I was nearly passing out from hunger. The Japanese seem be infinitely patient—or is that a stereotype?

At the entrance to the dining room, I noticed a woman standing next to the doors with her hands over her ears, I assumed, to try to keep out some of the NOISE: jukebox blaring, pinball machines clanging, and young people screeching and laughing. She suddenly crouched down next to the doors, her tense face turned away to the wall.

After several minutes of watching her be ignored, I wondered how much I'd freak her out if I went up to comfort her with my foreign face. Someone came at last, sat her in a wheelchair, gave her some cotton for her ears, and then took her away.

People around the world must quietly crack up all the time from the noise that crashes on their ears: traffic, music, voices, radios. It's especially awful here. That poor woman, absorbing it for all of us.

An old, craggy kimonoed gent joined me at my table at dinner. He said in English, "I sleeping" to my *"Osoi des ne?"* ("It's certainly late, isn't it?") I assumed he meant he'd been sleeping so he hadn't minded that dinner was served so late. Or that he's usually asleep by now. No telling what he thinks he heard *me* say.

Back in the state room, sipping sake offered by one of the young men, with a distinct chicken *katsu* aftertaste in my mouth. (Japanese version of Western cutlet.) I glanced through the guys' magazines, eight or nine of them, all girlie ones, all somewhat S/M, and foolish as hell. It's probably wise that I didn't show too much interest!

14

June 2, Saturday. On the Honshu-Hokkaido Ferry.

I ate breakfast with two middle-aged ladies from Osaka. They asked the usual: 1. Are you on a trip? 2. How long are you staying? 3. How long have you been in Japan? 4. Are you traveling alone? Followed by the usual comments: 1. Your Japanese is *jozu* (good). (It isn't, believe me.) 2. Your use of *hashi* (chopsticks) is *jozu*. (It isn't.) Plus many helpful sounds, ending in the proper *Osaki ni's (*Excuse us for leaving before you), handshakes, and pats on the back.

Several small groups of young teens, mostly girls traveling together, filled up the lounges between meals. One conspicuous group conspired to do all it could to gain the attention of everyone, especially young men within a half-mile radius.

Shrieking over card games, giggling, and shaking violently to the jukebox. When they managed to snare the attention of some male, the noise level suddenly settled down, and each one tried to appear composed, disinterested, and totally involved in the game.

All the grandmothers on board must sigh over these young girls. In their cutesy hats, bright shirts, jeans, and antics modeled after Japanese TV ads modeled after American TV ads, the girls closely resemble the teenage world of the American 1950s. Self-consciously pursuing some ideal of fun, they squeal and squirm, and undoubtedly know all the latest hit songs and current flip remarks. Centers of the universe, bright little pieces of fluff, which will, this being Japan, much too soon crumble into facsimiles of magazine wives, bound in print aprons with stainless steel kitchens at their backs.

I'm reading Shulamith Firestone on the 20th Century evolution of feminism. Does it show?

June 3, Sunday. Otaru-Sapporo.

The next day I passed up lunch, expensive and lousy. Japanese sausage, peanuts from the guys, and a Coke from the machine made a passable substitute. With yummy *onigiri* (rice balls) passed around at 5pm just before the ship began to think about docking.

More reading Shulamith, more chatting, more window staring, corridor strolling, and then a mad dash around 7 to prepare for arrival. With a set of right-on-time handshakes from all the fellows and *ogenki de's* (keep in good spirits) all around.

I went down with my *rukusaku* (backpack) to wait with all the endless groups of ladies. (*Rukusaku:* a "loanword" from the English and German *rucksack*. Hundreds of words have come into Japanese like this, such as *pan* (bread) from Portuguese *pao,* which came from 16th Century traders. True of every language, I'm sure.)

Three or four tour groups were headed up by an animated old man brandishing a fistful of red and yellow flags over his head and bellowing outrageous jokes, sending titters rippling through the crowd. At every whistle of the dock or ship, one old lady loudly roared, "*Oi!*" and all the others squealed and giggled. It went on endlessly. Too much, these old ladies.

I started chatting to a red-hatted, red-shirted, red-bagged, and red-lipsticked girl who turned out to be going to the same youth hostel, so we joined forces after docking and got a cab together. Later, several others from the ferry showed up at the hostel.

It was kind of funky and full of good feeling, the first time I'd stayed in one in Japan. An *obasan* (auntie) with no teeth directed the show from an *ippai* (full up) kitchen. The room was very unkempt, filled with skis, half-made pottery, felt

16

badges, tea cups, and shelf after shelf of cooking paraphernalia.

The living room also *ippai* with very lusty-lunged singers. I've always wondered why choruses seem like such a joke. It's because they are, that's why. That dreadful seriousness: "Let's get right down to business!" With a leader determinedly beating out the rhythm on the piano bench. What a sweet farce it was, with the entire kitchen help making wry faces at every high note.

At first, Red Hat and I were put into a first floor room where an older woman (who looked like a mountain peasant) and a young girl were talking about how it was early for the flowers that people come to this area to see in the summer.

After dinner, we were moved upstairs to the bunk room where all the struggling singers were sleeping. Red Hat found someone driving to Sapporo in the morning, good luck indeed.

The water in the traditional communal bath for women was from the mountains: freezing cold from the tap and too hot to enter in the tub. The tap was bound in a sand-filled kerchief to strain minerals. I knelt on the tile and managed to give myself an adequate washing up, but had no intention of entering that boiling cauldron. I've learned to love Japanese baths, but have my limits.

The chattering and card playing continued for some time downstairs, but I managed to fall asleep right away. Slept more soundly than in days. (How soundly could one sleep in a room with four grown men on a moving ferry?)

Then, I *crashed* awake at 4:30am when the sun exploded through the window. I managed to doze off again and got up at 6. (What a life—can this be me getting up so early?)

Several of us hiked up the hill behind the hostel while we waited for breakfast. (A problem with early mornings is that without the complicated morning toilette of the Japanese girls,

17

some of us are up and ready for breakfast ages before any others. I think the hostel managers actually wake the women half an hour before the men just for this reason.)

What a lovely view: down the long hill to the town below and out to the ocean and the rows of fog-bound ships lined up in blue and white. Across the field, a cluster of singers were already out, practicing scales and rubbing the sleep out of their eyes.

A cowbell rang and down the hill we ran. Eggs, toast, and, Lord bless us, coffee! Knowing foreigners well, the kind *obasan* had substituted fried eggs for me for the traditional raw one that I lie awake at night worrying about someday having to eat for breakfast in Japan.

In addition, she had prepared the same for Red Hat, I assume, so I wouldn't feel conspicuous. I did anyway. At any other time of day, I think I might be able to get a raw egg down, but first thing in the morning, never. I know it gets somewhat cooked in the hot rice, and I have eaten sukiyaki with sauce made with a raw egg, but still... .

Then I was off with Red Hat in the car, with waves and thanks to the *obasan.* I bet it would be fun to run a place like that. For a week or two.

The driver left us off at the bus station in Sapporo. I called a hostel to reserve the night's lodging and stowed the pack in the bus station luggage room.

Then I said goodbye to Red Hat, who was off to visit a friend. She was a funny, pouty-mouthed little thing. If it's true that people have a natural expression to their faces, hers was a cross between a teasing pout and bitter pout, both in keeping with the mask of the young Japanese woman.

It was all of 8:45am. I headed downtown, taking a peek at the prefectural building as I passed. Odd Western architecture but otherwise unexciting.

Then I walked in the direction of the Botanical Gardens of Hokkaido University, a perfect time before the Sunday crowds. Made a slow walk to the center, through azaleas, lilies, irises, pine, hemlocks, and discovered: Oh, my God, LILACS!

Millions of them! Rows and rows and rows! All in bloom! In a hundred different magnificent shades of purple, blue, and white. Lilacs! Like meeting a dear, old friend again!

I inhaled each perfect scent, sank my face into them, chewed on a few petals, and mumbled endearments from one bush to the next, making an absolute loony fool of myself all the way down one row and up the next. An orgy of lilacs! (Glad it was early and the gardens almost empty.)

Then I managed to compose my shattered self and went along quietly to the swamp areas. Shrubs, pines, hickories, and then back to those lilacs! They are everything to me! Childhood, homesickness, womanhood, love, death, birth, and heaven itself! Lilacs! Never will I go so far from them again. Life itself, lilacs! (No one will believe a word of this, but it's true.)

Further along, rock gardens, medicinal gardens, greenhouses, and a very strange Ainu museum with walls and walls of stuffed birds. (Gross, I tell you, gross!) Most contrary to natural laws and I wondered why they didn't have the taxidermist himself in there along with his dog and someone else's horse. Yuck!

I walked downtown towards the Odori Park, the main square, but didn't know where it was until I got to the middle of it. Buzzed around the shopping arcades for a bit, then found some lunch.

Life seems pretty good here: low pollution, high living standard, and not the extremes as in parts of Tokyo. Plus I'm getting very few stares and little notice of my *gaijin* face.

19

It feels as if there's enough here for most of the population. This may be why they can accept each other as human beings and *gaijins* get the same. It's nice for a change.

There was the same feeling on the southern island of Kyushu. But one cannot depend on it. The golden clouds of the foreign land can easily be collapsed by one unexpected creep screaming, *"Gaijin!"* at the top of his (or her) lungs. Though, it has been nice to let the reins loose for a time.

With a roaring blister on my heel, I walked back to the station for the backpack. Bought some bandaids and a copy of *Newsweek,* a shameful indulgence but the cultural disparity is fun.

I wanted to sit on the grass in the park with all the Sunday families, but by that time it was getting chilly. So I spent the 20-minute wait for the bus sitting on a bench at the bus station reading about Watergate wives.

The bus passed by a famous park I'd thought of going to, but Sunday crowds like that I don't need. Would also have liked to see one of the Sapporo temples.

There are few temples in Hokkaido since it was missionary territory, unlike Kyoto. One of the largest is the Sapporo Japan Temple run by the Mormons.

My Canadian friend, Duncan Frewin, in Kyoto, who loaned me a Hokkaido guidebook, was right, Sapporo is pretty much of a dud, except for those LILACS. That's all I need for a shrine!

At the end of the bus route, we could see the hostel further up the hill, a large imposing cement building that looked very much like a YWCA. Another hosteller joined me on the hike up.

He was from Kochi, with somewhat typical freaked-out *gaijin* reactions (ho hum). Halfway up we got rides with some guys on motorcycles, verrrry beeeg ones too, all the way up to the front door. I generally disapprove of motorcycles, so dangerous, but it was a cool way to arrive at the hostel.

The place was full of various young people who had all spent time in Kansas and others who had a ball calling for "Miss Mi-cher-ru" (Miss Mitchell) over the loudspeaker. Annoying, but harmless.

Others said, "I want to go to America" and then didn't say another word all evening as they slouched down in front of the TV with their American T-shirts and long hair.

I got put in a bunkroom for eight. Much different and more institutional than last night's lodging. Hope there are others more like that.

June 4, Monday. Sapporo-Asahikawa-Sounkyo Gorge.

I went out for a smoke to the TV area last night and in walked Miss Red Hat from the last hostel. Also a foreigner, a blond, older man who looked potentially real, someone I could talk to.

During dinner we caught each other's eye and nodded. Just nodded. I thought, ah, very fine, and very Japanese. But I was mistaken. He caught the rest of me later and talked English manically as if he hadn't used it in days, which was probably true. He was Danish, so it wasn't even his native language. His eyes were almost blank, a demeanor one must get from fending off stares for too long. A bit creepy.

He'd been traveling alone for seven months on a vacation from his farm and had spent two years at some other time in his life in the United States on a farm out West. Long complicated stories of Thailand, America, Australia, and Hong Kong, ships to every place you could imagine. How he surprised some girls in a bath in Osaka and what he did when someone came at him with a knife in Macao. The Japanese boy who'd been to Kansas stood behind us telling all his

21

friends in loud Japanese how that's the way it is, people of the same race always have so much to say to each other. Huh?

The Dane nailed me again after dinner and during the meeting, stories ooooozing out of him, desperate for contact, bizarre and yucky indeed. He made a rather conspicuous show of getting directions from the Japanese girls during the song fest. I chose to ignore the typical *gaigin* male display, but was embarrassed anyway.

A pleasant group was staying at that hostel. One looked like my favorite revolutionary student in Kochi must have looked as an undergraduate, the same lanky hair falling over his forehead, the offhand manner, and the "student-worker" veneer. Which will completely disappear in a couple years into the *salariman* (salary man) image.

The singing was a riot. Lots of individual choruses and silly ribaldry. Ridiculous, loveable creatures, these young guys, who have so little time before they grow up and become serious businessmen and oppressive husbands. Despite their present antics, foolishness, and the naturalness with which they wash their own dishes.

As soon as the *gaijin* walks in, everyone's determined to sing English songs even though no one knows more than the first line of *The Greenu Greenu Grassu of Ho-mu*. (Come to think of it, that's about all I know of any typical camp song.)

I really would have preferred to be up in the bunkroom leisurely reading Firestone. Harumph. This mandatory good-spirited business could get to be a drag one of these days.

I went to bed around 11pm and was up at 7am to more lovely weather. How long can it last? Breakfast with Mr. Denmark and then out with two girls to catch the bus downtown. Incredible early morning view from the hill. Very much like Ohara yesterday, only instead of ocean, a cover of city smog.

At the station, the girls headed me in the direction of my train and then left for Wakkanai, the northernmost tip of Hokkaido.

The train ride to Asahikawa lasted two hours with an old lady in a kimono sitting next to me. She spent the whole time pointing at my legs and telling everyone within earshot how much more comfortable jeans are than kimono for traveling. With a shy young couple across from us nodding at everything she said.

At Asahikawa I left the backpack on the train platform for Kamikawa and skipped out in the half hour wait for a cup of coffee. (Could you leave a pack on an American train platform for half an hour?)

Bought some bread and cheese for a train snack, boarded, and found a seat next to a worker who said he was also going to Sounkyo Gorge for a holiday.

When we arrived, he got me to the right bus, which was full of other tourists. Who else would be going to the middle of a mountain range in June?

Incredible mountain scenery all along the way. The clear glass ceiling of the bus gave the full effect of waterfalls, huge craggy rock cliffs, and pine trees.

At the bus center, I headed towards a phone to call the farmhouse hostel I'd chosen at random out of the guide book. I found two girls already phoning another hostel. I quickly changed my mind and asked them to please call their hostel back and reserve for me too.

In such situations, I sometimes wonder if I'm guilty of taking advantage of the Japanese "niceness," but they were glad to do it and I was very appreciative. Plus they got to practice a little English and me a little Japanese.

Then we all walked up the trail to the hostel: 500 feet straight up through mud and brambles to a highway and then another 500 feet to the little stone hostel. It was right next to a very elegant European-looking hotel with balconies for the great view.

We signed in, left our bags, and used the toilets. In the unisex john, I found some graffiti obviously written by a *gaijin* male and most likely an American: "I am really horny and want to get laid and Japanese pussy doesn't give out. And I want to get stoned. When are the Japanese going to discover grass and acid?"

Kimochi ga waruiiiii!! (Very bad feeling!) It made me think of Harold, Harvey, and all the other not-so-dear foreign male sexists I've known here. God, what bull. Yuck!

Before heading for the rope tow to the top of the mountain, the two girls and I got some ramen to boost our energy and talked over the steamy noodles. They were both college dropouts, as have been several other girls I've met on the trip. Most of them are just waiting around to get married, some working in the meantime.

It seems as if those who have the guts to go off traveling by themselves, or in small groups like this, are always friendly and much more interesting than the students I had in my classes in Kochi. Those girls just sat at home studying cooking, *koto* (zither), tea ceremony, and English in preparation for marriage. Then again, perhaps small trips to Hokkaido are part of the marriage prep course now.

The rope tow was expensive, 500 yen (about $1.60), but well worth it. We went all the way to the TOP of the world—*honto!* (really!)—into piles of snow, but packed down and dirty from thousands of tourists' feet.

We climbed around, whooping it up in the snow, and trying to avoid all the picture takers. We took each others' pictures and then that of a young couple who wanted someone to take theirs after they'd each taken one of the other (all very Japanese). Damned cameras, what a drag they can be here.

24

Then down to the viewing area and the scenic-as-hell view (*honto* again). There were far too many people, but that's fairly predictable, and I doubt as bad as midsummer.

Now back at the hostel, rather like the one last night, very businesslike and linoleum on all the floors. To dinner and the delightful *onsen* (hot spring bath).

June 5, Tuesday. Sounkyo Gorge-Akan-Lake Mashu-Kucharo-Shari-Utoro.

My dear, you've had a busy day. Jeesh.

After dinner and bath last night, I spotted some *gaigin kami* (hair of the foreigner). This fellow, a Londoner, had arrived in Japan a few weeks ago with the Royal Shakespeare Troupe, decided the Tokyo climate was not to his liking, and set off with his backpack and fancy camera for the northern regions.

He was reading *Alice in Wonderland* to "keep up the structures of the English language," he said. "So I won't forget, you know." Huh?

Lots of English words spilling over. How manic we *all* get! This guy was an improvement over the Dane though, less desperate, and his hearing not quite as impaired. By trade, a London printer, he was cool, young, worldly, and naïve at the same time, smart and cocky.

Both of us had lots of nervous energy to talk, and I found myself feeling nervous. The whole thing of outer-ness, how we appear to others, and I suppose I really DO look the part of the English teacher on holiday. But one does rather dislike the conclusions you know he's coming to about who you are and what your world is like. On the other hand, "English teacher on holiday" probably protects me from being hit on, and that's ok with me.

Yes, it's going to be strange indeed returning to the world of Western men again after being ignored or head-tripped for so long as an oversized version of Margaret Mead.

So this morning, I didn't rush downstairs to take him up on his offer to hitch to Abashiri together. Saw him leave, went back for a cigarette and some strong *bancha* tea, and then left about 7:15am.

Hiked down the path and out to the highway. Beautiful, full, enormous, and superb as gorges go. Hiked with great spirit for about a kilometer, then the pack magically got about 20 kilos heavier.

So I decided to hitchhike. Had thought I wouldn't. Females alone can be *chotto abunai* (a little dangerous). But what the hell, guys can do it, and anyway, this backpack's heavy and the road's a long way ahead. (You can see I did considerable thinking on the subject.)

In about five minutes, a diesel truck stopped, and I leaped in. Was really surprised to have a truck stop, and I think the driver was surprised himself. We chatted all the way up the road for about two hours.

Then he stopped, I got out, bought a Coke, and was off to hitchhike again, a car stopping right away. This time the driver was a funny, quiet little man who kept the radio on full blast and said twice how it must be lonely traveling by oneself, encouraging my nervousness considerably.

He left me at the Kitami bus station. (We had passed the Londoner hitching along the way. Early birds catch the what?)

I checked out the bus schedule, one in an hour, 420 yen (about $1.30). Then went off across the street to a coffee shop for the morning indulgence and the making up of the mind.

My friend Penny, an American physical therapist in Kochi, was so damned right about traveling alone: greater

26

freedom, no one else's whims and moods to accommodate, and you can be as lazy or as disciplined as you want. Most good.

I decided to hitch and save the yen. The town was dry and dusty, making hiking a very dry drag.

Finally two guys stopped. They were going in the direction of Abashiri, but I ended up going along with them to the Akan National Park, Lake Kucharo, and Lake Mashu.

They were both policemen, one very quiet, and I thought the whole time that he was pissed at his friend for stopping, until the end when his shyness thawed.

I didn't have any idea where we were and thought we were still headed for the northeast coast when we reached the first famous lake. Kucharo was enormous with a huge sloping rock observation area and lots of those 10 yen viewing machines.

Several Ainu men and women were sitting around posing with stuffed bears so the tourists could take pictures.

Look! Look! Everyone look! Look! Climb on the rocks! Look some more! Take pictures from 15 different angles! One of me with him and him with him, and the other him with me! And then the three of us! Snap! Snap! Snap! Snap! Buy Cokes! And back in the car!

The lake was very beautiful, but so far down below through the trees that you had a hard time being touched by it. A pity that you can't get right down near it.

But then again, that's probably a damned good thing for the lake because if you could, it too would have been covered with litter long ago like Mount Fuji. But this "Scenery" business with a capital "S" is so removed—I want it HERE!

They left me off in Bihoru with many *kiotsukete's* (be careful!), etc., and I barely had time to get to the other side of the road and look the part, when a car stopped. A funny little man (the world abounds with them, at least this world) going beyond Shibetsu halfway to Shari.

He didn't say much the whole time. We shared a chuckle over a kid stopped by the cops, but that was all. He left me across from a restaurant where he was going in to deliver something.

I followed him in for a bowl of Sapporo miso ramen, renowned in this area. The whole time, he disavowed any knowledge of the strange foreigner.

Everyone in the place was otherwise occupied anyway, watching a horrible TV show about rape victims turning into vampires. Enough to make anyone lose their lunch, but somehow fitting in with reading Firestone. I managed to take my bowl of noodles off in a corner and sit with my back to the blaring machine.

Back to the road and got a lift right away with two fellows in a sports car. Both young and the driver absurdly hip, with dark glasses and long hair.

The passenger fell asleep five minutes later. It must be quite a novelty to go out for an afternoon drive and pick up *gaijins,* enough to make you want to get out of the house.

They left me off at the Shari station. I'd decided to go to an obscure hostel in Iwabetsu, halfway up the side of the peninsula on the guide map, but no telephone listed.

So instead, I tried one in Utoro, but couldn't seem to get through. The bus driver tried to help, but couldn't get through to me.

Finally I looked up and there was Camera Boy from last night's hostel, saying, "You dial the first four numbers, wait for the dial tone, then the last two." Oh.

Then he said he was going to another hostel in Utoro and why didn't I go there too. Always open to suggestion, especially when it means being watched over for a bit, I agreed. I dialed successfully this time and just as soon as I

28

said my name, they shouted, in smart-aleck English, "Okay! Okay!" Great. One of *those* places.

I'd thought of trying to hitch to Utoro, but began to feel comfortable with his company, so took the bus.

So the two of us sat on the bench and waited for the bus. He bought ice creams and told me all about taking pictures of swamp birds.

Finally, after what seemed ages, we piled on the bus and took off for the hills. And what hills!

Snow-peaked with wide clear ocean below. *Sugoi!* (Wow!) Cliffs, peaks, fjords, and islands jutting up in rocky faces and pines just off the shore. We drove through a series of fishing villages: Nets out drying, glass bulbs strewn about, fish laid on racks, and sturdy weather-beaten houses like those in Gloucester, Massachusetts, or Boothbay, Maine.

Schoolchildren kept getting off the bus to run home to farms or fishing huts. Lovely country. And a great bus ride, complete with a running commentary on area high points and famous local songs rendered off-key by our perky lady guide.

We arrived after a long, long ride. What do you expect for 420 yen? We were met by the hostel micro-bus which took us several miles straight up.

These youth hostels are always stuck way the hell in some beautiful spot that's a bitch to get to. (But I bet few other *gaijins* make it to this one.)

We were greeted loudly by three more kids from last night's hostel, one of them with me three nights in a row now. This certainly must be The Great Hostel Circuit we're on.

We all tromped in, removed boots in the front entryway, signed in, complete with giggles in English (theirs) and wobbly show-off Japanese letters (mine), put away the packs, down to eat, then write, chat, managed to miss the meeting, and now a bath and zzzzzz.

Tomorrow, a Zen temple and quiet?

June 6, Wednesday. Utoro-Shari-Kucharo-Mashu-Teshikago-Nishibetso-Nemuro.

I remember saying something last night about hoping for a Zen Temple and quiet. Didn't quite make either the temple or the coast, but almost had enough quiet.

Woke up out of a dream I couldn't remember, especially since it was 5am and three giggling girls were whispering about going on a walk. They left and returned at 6 waking me up for good. Said they were "ascared to go." (It had to translate like that.) I just groaned out of bed and got to the day. Breakfast with Camera Boy.

The egg turned up raw and I ended up asking to have it cooked a bit. This keeps presenting such a problem.

Breakfast eggs in Japan are always raw; I am never able to face it and always wonder if one just ought not to eat an egg at all in such a case. Or perhaps the solution would be just to eat the damned thing! Heavens, what a thought.

After all, it isn't as if you just crack one end and take it straight or even with a little whiskey as a hangover cure. You crack it on top of your bowl of steaming rice, add a little soy sauce, and mix it all up with your chopsticks. The egg supposedly ends up slightly coddled, and mixed up with all that soy sauce and rice, you hardly notice it's there. (Ha!)

But right after waking up? And they don't get coddled all that much.

Frankly, watching all the Japanese kids deal with a raw egg first thing in the morning has not made me like the idea any better.

I left with Camera Boy for the bus stop down the hill. He really was a cute one and maybe liked me a little too.

We had a good talk about traveling alone and I told him all the silly questions people ask. He cracked up when I told him that everyone thinks my Japanese is good, but it's only because they always ask the same questions.

30

He was a great relief from the foolish hostel boys, patronizing and silly with their cutesy English. I keep trying to ignore them but it's hard since they're so obvious. That's the way one must get, stuck way up here in the boonies, without contact with the real world.

The bus was a half-hour wait, so I decided to hitch instead and walk along the shore. Said goodbye to my companion and started off.

Hiked up the road a way and then walked between the fishing houses down to the ocean wall. Wide, clear water—out, out, and out! I climbed down to the edge and dabbled my hands in it. Ah, the ocean!

Dipped my hands, drenched my face—great invigorating smells. Filled my pockets with lucky stones and said good morning to the fishermen laying out their nets. One woman was dumping tied bundles of something into an enormous steaming pot over a fire pit.

Then back up to the road again. More hiking and hitching. No rides came, so I rounded the pass and went back down to the water.

Took off one layer of clothes; the day was warm already. Lay out on the rocks at the edge of the water and just stayed there in the middle of it all. Then leaped around on the rocks for a few minutes, shrieked and squealed and tossed and danced. Just a little of each though. Fishermen started coming in to dip for kelp, so I thought I should take off for the road again.

Finally got picked up by a funny little guy whose colloquial Japanese I couldn't understand. What's more, he couldn't understand much of my standard textbook stuff either. After five minutes, he realized he'd forgotten his bag and back we went to Utoro.

A two-minute wait while he ran in for it, and then off again. He wanted to let me, the well-traveled foreigner, know that his company had a branch in Osaka, equivalent to New York City for a down-Mainer. Everyone wants to tell you something.

I got left near the Shari post office, sent letters and cards, then went off to a coffee shop near the station for the morning coffee. With *whipped* cream! I was just about to wonder why anyone should have to pay so much and wait so long, when the treat arrived.

I got pointed in the right direction out of town by the waitress and hitched a ride quickly from two young guys in a white sports car. Turned out we'd all been on the ferry together coming over.

They were headed for Lake Mashu and Kucharo. I'd hoped to get a ride past there since I'd done both the day before, but since I'd forgotten to buy postcards, I shrugged my shoulders and said I was willing to take it in twice. (Bet I'm one of the few travelers—*gaijin* or Japanese—to see the lakes twice in one trip!)

I was glad I did. We stopped on the other side of Kucharo, and I struck up a pleasant conversation with one of the Ainu men. He'd been sitting all day with a small bear in a fenced-off area so the tourists could take pictures of him. Nice eyes.

We talked about the hot sulfur springs and how they use it for central heating in Iceland. Both of us are foreigners by Japanese standards, but actually in Hokkaido, the Japanese are the foreigners.

I thought afterwards that I would have liked to have said something about this to him, how the Japanese came in and took over the Ainu land. But perhaps it's better I didn't. It might have been taken as rude. (Or at least by Japanese standards, it probably would have been, and they're the ones who make the rules here.)

The two guys were interesting traveling companions, young and sexy. I had a passing thought that they might be gay, but also noticed lipstick-stained butts in the ashtray.

One of them "draws kimonos." I didn't quite get that. It must mean he designed the fabric. The other was a carpenter. Brothers from Kyoto. I bought Cokes for all of us and then forgot to use the available toilet and soon discovered the *cardinal* rule of the road: "Pee whenever you can." I didn't get another chance until two hours later, the gorgeous scenery of that whole time nothing but a blur, blinded by throbbing kidneys.

They let me off near Teshikaga. I would have headed right then and there for the woods, but there wasn't one secluded spot to be seen. (And I was not, thought I, about to bare me *gaijin* bum to the world!) Rides were coming so fast, there was no chance to pee—hard to believe.

Was about to head for the woods after the next ride, when a diesel truck pulled up. I wasn't even hitching, for crying out loud. Oh, what the hell, I took it anyway.

Let it be known: trucks bounce one *hell* of a lot. Besides which, the roads were unpaved most of the way and under construction every few miles; this coupled with unusually poor suspension in both the truck and me. Ghastly.

Finally was able to get out in Nishibetsu right in front of a ramen shop. I staggered in and asked to use the toilet. Sigh. Very nearly burst into tears when I couldn't get my boot laces undone in the entryway to walk barefoot through the shop to get to the *benjo* (toilet).

Had some delicious *shio* (chicken broth) ramen. That's three days of ramen, have got to start altering this diet, though it's famous up here and delicious. The hostel meals are a bora galore; one at least needs an interesting lunch. I might even consider adding toast (!) to tomorrow's morning coffee.

Just as I was thinking this, the *obasan* (proprietor) brought me a plate of local shrimp. People are so kind here; sometimes it shakes me up. I learned early never to compliment anything in someone's house or they'd give it to you.

Heavens, I couldn't even remember how to ask her in Japanese, "How do you eat something like this?" But the puzzlement on my face communicated itself adequately and she showed me. Very *oishiii!* (delicious!)

Bought some crackers, chocolate, and smokes at a store across the street. It certainly seemed as if I was the first *gaijin* they'd ever seen. But it was less rude than charming: wide mouths, stares, just looking. I wasn't made to feel like a freak and the devil herself, as in other places.

Back to the road. Got a ride right off in a pickup truck. The driver hoisted the backpack into the back where it bounced around and picked up grease stains all the way to Nemuro. Strange little man.

He kept fiddling with the signal switch, talking fast and jerkily, in Tohoku dialect I couldn't understand. He had equal trouble with my textbook Japanese. Most peculiar.

He was going to Nemuro, that part I got. Then I gave answers that seemed appropriate and we both slowed down, repeating ourselves and getting down to what must have been more or less baby talk on both sides. Then that petered out to silence.

The roads began to get incredibly bad again. The biggest constancy of the day was rolling windows up against the dust. I didn't think I'd ever get enough water to wash out the thirst.

A most peculiar ride. Both of us quiet, me wondering a bit. Not being able to talk to someone can be *heavy*.

We arrived at the road to Nemuro, and he said something about going off on a side road, coming right back, and then heading for Nemuro. I got the *kaeru* (coming back) part and like a damned fool, nodded agreement.

At which point we shot off at an honest-to-God breakneck speed along the worst road I've been on in my life. Speeding alongside a set of tracks with a coal train puffing ahead, filling the air all around with dark rotten smoke. (I paused just long enough to understand why trains were considered devils when they first appeared.)

We went on, and on, and on, flying by farms, huge green fields, and school children trudging home, all left behind in a cyclone of dust. I gripped my bag with one arm and Duncan's precious guide book in the other and held on for dear life.

After about a minute of this—it seemed like 20—the terror really began to set in. Where the hell *were* we? Here I was headed surely for my doom encased in a rattletrap truck with a weird little guy I couldn't even talk to, careening further and further into nowhere. The gig was up, your luck's held out too long.

Even if he didn't sell you into white slavery or rape you, he'd probably chop you up into little pieces. And who will ever find you way out here in the sticks? (Truly my friend Sandra *may* start to worry about a week from now.)

I thought he can have my money and he can even fuck me—just get me out of here alive, dear God! And even if I didn't get raped or mutilated, I was surely going to be shaken to death tearing down this awful road!

Historic female tactics loomed in my mind. Screaming and crying might just get me out of this. I had an hysterical desire to look down at the life line on my right palm to see if it still says I'm going to live a long and oh-so-fruitful life.

Just as I was about to break into a sopranic wail, he shifted gears, slowed down, pulled into a small row of houses alongside a rural train station, and stopped in front of one of the rundown houses. Four runny-nosed kids and a woman were sitting out front.

I very nearly burst into tears right there. It was his home, and he was either on a legitimate errand or more likely, wanted his wife and kids to see the *gaijin* he'd found. The woman and I exchanged bows through the windshield, and then I got out and said hello.

Feeling like the picture of a World War II Red Cross worker in *The World Book Encyclopedia* I grew up with, I gave the kids some chocolate and picked up a squally one when he fell over on his bicycle from staring at me so hard. The bike was the only shiny object around.

It was about the worst poverty I've seen in Japan. Granted I've been insulated, leading a *gaijin* life, but it isn't exactly something your Japanese host would think of including in a typical tour.

Plastic sheets at the windows. Children covered with sores and insect bites. The oldest boy about six, a blank look in his eyes.

A younger child was inside without clothes on, too shy to look out or take any chocolate. Very spare rooms with the TV blaring a *Time* cracker commercial. The dusty front yard ran into a pitted dirt road between the houses, all lined up the same, like American migrant camps.

Thoughts later of how I might meet another foreigner that night at the hostel, how we'd exchange stories, and I'd relate this one. How much a game it can be, who can tell the most outrageous story. American liberal slumming.

But I was there in it, they knowing me, me knowing them, both of us discovering the other. It was not something at arm's length, to look at curiously, take data on, and make nice, neat, anthropological conclusions about. I may write it, and I may tell it, but I hope it will be told as something that the person telling was one with.

So then back we went to Nemuro, still silent and still bumpy, but much, much calmer, on my part at least. We drove across a flat, reedy lagoon area into the town.

Then the bay opened up, and I nearly did laugh and cry with joy. A whole village of fishing homes, set close together before the sea, nets and drying fish lit up by the afternoon sun.

Then into the town. He said, "*Doko*?" ("Where?") and I said, "*Eki*" ("Station"), so that's where I ended up. Exhausted, with an interesting adventure behind me and a grease-stained backpack.

The city of Nemuro was generally dusty and poor. No sidewalks to speak of, which I've gathered is a Western expectation, but it still spells poverty to me.

Walked over to the hostel, a rather grubby little one with a posh looking *ryokan* (inn) on the other side supposedly for the richer travelers. It seemed like the inn's old *futons* (mattresses), chopsticks, and other second-hand junk must be sent over for the hostel kids.

First, a bath and then dinner. After, I took an evening walk with a girl who was also on her own. We went down to the water to eat ice cream and watch the sun set. These towns remind me of places like Biddeford, Maine. Old factory towns devolved into industrial wastelands.

But I was glad I decided to stop here. It wasn't exactly one of the hot spots on the hostel circuit. Not a place where one was apt to meet kids from other hostels or other foreign creatures. A nice relief.

There was a distinct absence of even a pretense of the hostel gung ho spirit. Very pleasant to be spared that for one night. Not even any Red Hat or Camera Boy to chat with.

This chatting in Japanese is rather astounding me. I really *am* living in Japanese for the first time in the two years I've been here. For three straight days, I have spoken nothing but Japanese.

Actually it's not all that unusual; lots of foreigners live entirely within the culture, some of them (especially men) taking great pride in their abilities to assimilate. But fortunately or unfortunately, I've never had to.

There's always been some English-speaking student or other foreigner around. I never thought I could until now. But I am good, dammit, I really am, or good enough.

Of course I'm not having any earth-shattering discussions, but still, getting around and keeping up my half of a conversation is something. Though, I do find that I'm talking English to myself sometimes, hollering, "All right now, I'm ready!" up the empty road to bring rides.

But it's okay and fun and a good time is being had by all. Such good luck I'm having too—rides, weather, timing.

June 7, Thursday. Nemuro-Akkeshi (Kokutai-ji Temple), Kushiro-Obihiro.

This is being written to the most annoying accompaniment of *Puff the Magic Dragon* sung by Peter, Paul, and Mary and that crummy little news and carol bit by Simon and Garfunkel. The students here love them.

I just wish I knew how to disconnect the damned speakers in this enormous cafeteria. It isn't piped into the dorm area, but I can't smoke there so I'll have to put up with this.

So today: The day first started at 5am when those inevitable early-rising females decided to go for one of their walks or some such nonsense. I pulled back the bunk curtain, found out what time it was, groaned, and turned over. Bah!

Coupled with a SPLITTING headache, of the hangover variety, but heavens, I haven't had a drop in days. Finally rolled out, half-blind, around 7am, head blasting.

Down to breakfast with fears of that raw egg. But behold: boiled! A thousand blessings on our invisible host who must have set it all up before rushing off to work. With marvelous, remarkable toast that we browned ourselves on top of a huge stove in the middle of the room.

I ate with the girl I'd met yesterday. After breakfast we sat talking a while, and I told her the story of the strange ride yesterday. I wanted to share it with someone and she was special enough in her own way.

Then we both took off. She to the bus depot and me out to hitch, headache blaring. My eyes were sensitive as hell to the light. The headache must have been due to over-exposure from sun glare and the ocean yesterday.

I figured I'd better buy some sun clips at the first opportunity, much as I hate the tourist image. Just about every foreign tourist I've ever seen in Japan wears sunglasses. It gives us such a look of haughty distance from the world around us.

But pain and blindness are not acceptable. A sun hat and sunglasses are essential for all the tromping about I've been doing.

As a result of headache pain, I do not clearly remember either ride that morning. Both drivers were full of the Tohoku dialect of this area, funny, and hard to understand.

I got left off in the center of Akkeshi and walked down in the direction of the business section. No sidewalks, dusty, small, and poor. Went into a drugstore to ask for sun clips.

The druggist didn't have them, but sent his daughter with me to the local optical shop around the corner. They cost 800 yen (around $2.60), but the clerk gave me a 100-yen discount.

Then to a coffee shop for the morning indulgence and a liberal dose of aspirin. I could hardly enjoy the coffee through the pain. Really awful.

With shaded eyes, I headed off in the direction of the bridge to the other half of town, an island with a Zen temple I wanted to visit. Got a ride with a couple across the bridge, right up to the front gate.

I left the pack next to a pine tree and walked inside. A beautiful, peaceful spot. Pine trees, statues, and a small house with a garden in front. I climbed a path and could see across to temple buildings with TV antennae on top. Rather a strange combination.

Further up, the path wound around and out with superb views of the harbor locked in with fog. Wonderful, green, purring fog. I reached the top and came out on a huge garden laid out against the sea, with a backdrop of bushes and sky. I carefully picked my way across looking for a path back down the other side.

Didn't find one but did scare what might have been a deer. Feeling very Zen about it all, everything one, and me and it and we and yes. Expected several robed monks to walk out of the woods and start hoeing.

What a beautiful little harbor down below. Fishing boats bobbing around close to the shore, nets out, clothes drying, and lines of fish.

I wandered about and came across what must have been a *zendo* (meditation room) at one time, with an old cemetery behind it. I sat on my haunches in the doorway of the zendo and looked at all the things around the room: Sutra book of chants, a well-used *kyosaku* (stick) for encouraging flagging sitters, the *obosan zabuton (*cushions especially for the master), and old dated scrolls, everything faded and slightly water stained. Lovely good feeling place to bow to with *gassho (*respect).

When I tried to walk around in the cemetery, I got menacingly swooped out by crows, very spooky. There were several red-roofed buildings under construction among the trees on the hillside above, but the area was roped off for construction.

While I was sitting on the garden stones eating lunch, the *obosan* (head priest) came out of his house and walked to the *zendo* with a dog.

I'd thought the place would be a lot bigger, that I might be able to do some *zazen* (meditation), or even stay the night, but it'd begun to look less and less like the guidebook's dated description.

After I finished my cheese and bread, I finally screwed up my courage, went over to introduce myself to the *obosan,* and was invited in for tea. I was ushered into the living room where his wife sat watching TV. We drank glasses of sweet cider and red birthday rice.

"Whose birthday?" I asked.

I think she said, "The temple God."

They kept offering food—pickles, candy, and a banana. I was sorry that I had nothing to share with them, but took out a packet of photographs of Kyoto and my family.

The *obosan* knew Kobori Roshi in Kyoto, the Zen teacher I studied with. And I think he said it ought to be possible to live in Hokkaido when I said I'd like to. It was a very pleasant visit, leaving me feeling a bit guilty because I'd hoped something nice like that might happen. I walked backwards out of the yard, with many bows and *ogenki de's* (be well).

Then I walked down to the bus stop. The bus had just gone, according to a woman who had also just missed it. We walked together a way, she with a baby on her back and me with my pack. We had a chuckle about the fact that my pack must be just as heavy as her kid.

As cars came along, I stuck my thumb out and, after a couple minutes, got a ride with a garage mechanic going all the way to Kushiro. *Yokatta! (*Great!) He sped along, lapping up great long stretches of ocean road.

We got to Kushiro; the driver said he wanted to stop at his friends' house first and then would take me to a good hitching place. The friends were carpenters, young and cute, working on a model house. He went in, probably to tell them about the foreigner he'd found, and then came out and invited me in.

Since the house was under construction, we didn't have to leave our shoes in the *genkan* (entryway); the first (and only) time I ever walked in a Japanese house with my shoes on. In fact, at the *gasshuku* (student rooming house) in Kyoto, my US handmade leather sandals were stolen from the *genkan*. A scandal to the foreigners living there!

The young men were all funny about having a foreigner there, the usual bit, but okay. My driver went and got a crab from his car, and we all stood around sucking on crab legs and tossing the shells in the shavings on the floor.

Then we went back to the highway. He left me in a really bad place for hitching, difficult for cars to stop easily.

But finally a guy stopped. He spoke English, had lived in Sacramento a couple years, and proceeded to give me a good old American lecture on hitchhiking. It made me rather nervous, especially when he implied that I was exploiting Japanese kindness to women. (I wonder where they keep it all?)

He kept saying, "I just can't see it, a woman hitchhiking by herself. Terrible, terrible." But it all had to be calmly spoken because he didn't have enough English to get really excited, for which I was grateful.

As we passed through the bridge at Kushiro, the whole area was covered in thick fog, very creepy, right in keeping with what he was saying. Yucky *kimochi* (feeling).

He left me off finally with many admonitions, and it took some time to get the next ride. There I was, out hitching in front of a little grocery store with half the town standing around giving advice on the cars that passed.

Little old ladies in kimonos were saying, "No, no, you don't want that one. That's just Grandpa Tajima going home," and so on. Back-seat hitchhikers? Really funny.

It was all a bit shocking to these grandmas, but I think they kind of dug it too. With a lot of *kiotsu-kete's* (be careful). They wished me well, even if they didn't overdo it too much.

Finally got away from the cheering squad and tried hitching next to a construction site with grinning middle-aged workers looking me up and down. I almost preferred the grandmothering.

At last a truck stopped, and the driver nearly proceeded to be the ride the last driver had predicted. Lots of questions he had no business asking, laughing in the wrong places, and sly little comments for which I declined to understand the language. Ha, ha indeed.

He let me off on the road to Obihiro. I had planned on getting beyond Cape Erimo, but doubted that many cars would pass that way on a weekday, there being nothing but scenery.

Somewhere in the midst of rides I had gotten myself headed in the direction of Obihiro, a fairly good-sized city in the middle of the island, instead of sticking to the coast as I had planned. I called a hostel from a filling station and got an okay for the night.

Back at the road, finally got a ride with a carpool of construction workers on their way home. Nice, simple, working men with decent questions, kindness, and good hearts.

I readily agreed with them that the Japanese work too hard, much more than American workers, and get paid a lot less. It was hard to keep up with their Japanese as I was feeling exhausted. Whizzed through some beautiful country: herds of cows, wide-open fields, and what they said were potato-packing factories (not so gorgeous). What a fine part of the world this is.

We went out beyond Obihiro to a small suburb where most of the workers lived. One had his car there and said he'd take me back into the city. I didn't quite understand all the logistics, but it felt safe and that's about all I cared about at that point.

So we all got out, and the two of us got into a shiny little gold sports car. Got a good look at the driver who'd sat quietly way in the back of the minibus. He was very nice looking, handsome, a calm face with nice eyes, and arms covered with black cloth bands from wrist to elbow for construction work. One of the more likeable Japanese men I've met this trip. (And a wedding ring on his left hand—I don't miss a thing.)

A pity to part, but there was the "Yu-su," (youth hostel), so out I got.

And what a place! After last night's cast-offs, this was the Hilton. And I was most definitely back on the hostel circuit again. A French girl and her Japanese boyfriend were sitting in the lobby, speaking gorgeous French. (Two years in high school and I should know?)

Funny, but when she and I came face-to-face in the bath later, we spoke Japanese to each other. (Doubt my French was up to it anyway.) And there were lots of young people I'd met earlier at other hostels.

I ate quickly, washed out some things, and got a bath. This has got to be one of the cleaner hiking trips I've ever been on! The young people in my bunk room found out I was an English teacher and were rather a drag about it. But they didn't keep up the "I am a girl!" bit too long, thank God, or I might just have killed one of 'em.

I went down to write and smoke in the lunch room, and a Japanese guy with a shaved head came in to talk. He spoke pretty good English, had been to Europe, and thought hitching was great. Another guy came in with less English and *champon Eigo/Nihongo* ensued. (Mixed English/Japanese, named for a seafood and vegetable soup famous in Nagasaki).

But it meant I had to write here in bed later instead of at a table with smokes. Ah, such is life. Ten o'clock to bed. And up at some equally unnatural hour.

June 8, Friday. Obihiro-Hiroo-Erimo Misaki-Shiraoi.

I woke up with those silly girls again, but rolled over for 30 more minutes. Finally went down for breakfast but it wasn't scheduled for another half hour. Damn girls.

So back up to the dorm to read *Newsweek* on the famine in Africa, India, and China. The worst in 60 years. Life is so easy here; we learn about suffering from magazines.

Ate (somewhat guiltily), packed, said goodbyes, and skedaddled out to the main road. Asked some high school kids the way to Hiroo and they said right. Walked a block and asked a shop owner. He said left. See, never trust anyone under 20! Harumph.

Got a ride quickly with a vegetable delivery man. Once again, I found we could barely understand each other's Japanese. He stopped at every little vegetable shop all the way from Obihiro to Hiroo.

He'd pull up in front of the shop, jump out, and stand at the back of the truck, saying, "*Tomato, wa*?" ("How about tomatoes?") chatting with all the spry ladies, flirting their heads off. (Even though I couldn't get every word, the body language and facial expressions were enough.)

At one stop, after he'd been gone for an especially long time, he came back with a handful of lilies-of-the-valley which he shoved over at me. What a sweet gesture. And a wonderful smell.

45

He let me off in Hiroo. I walked a way, found a shop, and got some sausage and cookies to go with my bread and cheese for lunch. I hitched alongside shop girls whizzing by on bicycles staring at the strange foreign apparition. Someday I swear I may be the cause of a major accident.

Finally got a ride with a man and his kid going to Samani. They decided part way to take me around by the Cape so I could get a look at it. He bought Cokes; I shared my cookies. The little girl was pleasant, not freaking out at having a *gaijin* sitting next to her. Nice to be around a decent kid again. Too much grownup life of late.

We all got out at the Cape and looked around. Even now in June, it was colder than hell. And what adjectives do we use now to describe such scenery? Magnificent, grand, etc. A frozen point of rocky cliffs jutting out into a raging sea. Miserable in winter, I'll bet. It's easy now to think how marvelous it would be to live here in Hokkaido, but I wonder about six months from now.

Then off again. None of us really understood our two versions of Japanese, lots of "Do you have a boyfriend?" questions, and the kid kept falling asleep on my yellow shawl. Lots of nice heads have fallen asleep on that shawl; it must be full of silky dream karma.

The roads were rotten as usual, and I began to find it rather scary to careen down the road with a kid asleep against my shoulder in the front seat, and of course no seat belts. The road was a rocky thread of dirt cut into the side of the cliff abutting the ocean. One skid and whole lot of us could have landed in the middle of the sea. But somehow we got through it unscathed.

I got out at the next town. Walked a way and then cut down to the ocean for some lunch. Sat up on a cement breakwater in view of the wide sea, with breaking waves and a good smell. Chopped off pieces of sausage and cheese with my trusty jack knife and downed it with the bread left over from yesterday's breakfast. Very delicious. Then back to the road for some coffee milk and out to hitch.

Got a ride in another truck between two of the more absurd men I've ever met. The passenger was hugging a red thermos on his lap and talking nonsense, at least as far as I could tell. The driver and passenger were hilarious clowns, both of them taking me seriously, but not quite believing it.

Conversation lingered several times right on the edge. Something I couldn't catch that sounded like "nembetsu." (Only definition on Google, "Mind of the Buddha," can't be right.)

Leading to "Like sex?" at which point, in order to maintain some level of sobriety, my Japanese and English both evaporated, and my attention became glued on the passing ocean scenery. Gentlemen both, but just barely, and I wouldn't have wanted to push it very far.

They began to run out of gas, and we all kept a desperate look out for a Standard station where they could use the company credit card. Finally had to stop at a Mobil.

The driver went off to the *benjo* (toilet), announced in a very loud voice, but came back right away. No toilet paper, also broadcast loudly.

And off again. Despite the horrible roads, I kept nodding and then being jolted awake by bumps. They finally let me off on a small road to town.

I ran down the hill to get a closer look at some beautiful race horses, but a car stopped right away with a young man and his father on their way to the next town. The kid had lived in California for a couple years, spoke good but wretchedly American English with all the "gonnas" and "yeahs."

I tried to get some information about the Aino out of him, this being really the first chance in days to ask questions in English. Unfortunately he seemed to get a little put out by my probing so I quit.

Then I got out and picked up a ride with an awful, awful laugher. He would ask questions, be real enough, and then break into this horrible, artificial laughter. A salesman and if he was any example, it's definitely a suspicious trade.

Out, and phoned the youth hostel in Shiraoi. Okay! Got a bus to town, but got off too soon and ended up on the edge of the next town.

The driver let me ride back with him to my stop while he explained the local custom of engaged couples bathing together in the hot-spring baths. This area appears to be one of the last strongholds of that lovely old custom.

But you wouldn't catch me in a coed hot spring, all those lecherous old men. I have enough trouble with little old grandmothers and 12-year-old-boys staring on the women's side.

Finally reached the hostel. Two Swiss girls were staying there, along with two Japanese girls from last night's hostel, and a guy I met in Sapporo. Small country this.

June 9, Saturday. Shiraoi-Muroman-Onuma.

Awoke the next morning suffering from distinct physical exhaustion. The morning headache persisted, so I had added eye drops to the backpack. But my eyes kept shutting anyway. Tired and bleary.

Life on the road begins to pale a little after a week. Walking back to the hostel this evening, I felt a strange juxtaposition of time and space. Standing there in the middle of all those trees, hills, and bridges, thinking, "I know I live here somewhere, and I can smoke in the bedroom, but where is it?"

I had a dream the other night that I'd been traveling down the coast of not Hokkaido but Maine. Similar shape in

48

some way. Today I half-imagined I was returning to the Portsmouth, New Hampshire, apartment of two years ago. Such is the cognitive dissonance of the transient mind. Oh my.

Perhaps it is time to be leaving Hokkaido. Got to get my feet back on "real" land again soon. This drifting about, vacation though it may be, does do funny things to your head after a while.

Early morning girls again, but this time I managed to sleep through them, not getting up until nearly 8am. In the dining room, my heart leapt at the sight of a jar of instant coffee. It turned out to belong to the Swiss girls. Oh, dear, a bit over-eager, but I did pass on my *Newsweek* to them. All's fair.

I sat drinking coffee and smoking until nearly 9, disgracefully lazy. But it felt good not to rush out predawn like an eager beaver Girl Scout. (Even though I was one myself. And proud of it!)

At last I went out with two sweet young girls to the nearby Ainu tourist village. What a horrible, rotten sell-out place. The Ainu were a beautiful people, strong, vibrant, in tune with nature, living on what they shot and fished, and involved in weaving, magic, and ceremonies.

Now, they are oddities to stare at alongside the bears, little round fluffy creatures who scratch themselves again and again so everyone will laugh.

The Ainu day, one would hope, will come again, but it's doubtful. There are no more than 10 or 11 thousand still living in Hokkaido, and now they are mostly farmers and fishermen.

Three or four demonstration houses were set up for walking through. Girls in Ainu dress sat around smoking cigarettes and drinking tea.

They took special pains to inform all comers that the old one over there was a real Ainu with a real painted Ainu tattoo around her mouth, 80 years old, would you believe. And hopefully, not understanding very much of what went on around her.

Outside were two long rows of shops, packed with cheap carvings, cutesy dolls, and all the other junk that goes with such a tourist show. The first and biggest shop had a big sign in English: "This is Chief Ashimoto's own shop. He has been to Hawaii two times." And one can only say, "So?"

Slightly depressed, I went back to the hostel. Some of the guys were out front working on a garden for the hostel parents. Really good feeling generally among the kids I've met at these places.

Yes, they might be drinking and smoking dope or any number of other "normal" things somewhere else, but there's no feeling at the hostel that sitting around drinking tea and singing songs is "kids' stuff" and none of that "As soon as the counselor's gone..." feeling in the air.

Like San Francisco in the late 1960s, you're friends from the first, until otherwise proven, no questions asked, and the young people are remarkably understanding and kind (with exceptions, of course).

Last night's meeting was a good example. Two very nice guys at either end of the table managed to entertain six self-conscious, shy girls for a long time in the light of the kerosene lanterns we were forced to use because the electricity was off.

The girls gave them little help, but will go home saying what a great time they had, only because two guys spent 2½ hours knocking themselves out being entertaining and friendly. At 10pm the lights came back on, and interestingly enough, the six girls suddenly doubled their animation.

Taking it slow this morning, I finally got off around 11am. A late start, but about time it were allowed. Got some lunch stuff at a market and set off.

Got a ride right off with two concrete-company workers, white collars and a bit stiff. I sat in the back seat and thought, "I'm never going to make this." Stomach really off, head a mess, and eyes burning to pop out. Then we dropped off the guy in the front seat and my getting in front improved things.

I got left off at Muroran on the highway to Onuma and the bay. The driver had hitched around Europe, so he insisted on making me a sign saying "Onuma" in great big lovely Japanese letters.

I got a ride soon after, with, of all delightful things, an ice cream truck! Have always wanted to ride in one. And it lived up to all my expectations: milk bars, coffee milk, popsicles, fudge bars, and the odd (to me) green tea ice cream on a stick.

We talked about the local scenic spots, and I said I was all for shooting straight through for home at this point. He thought it wasn't necessary for me to see Muroran, but to miss the lake up the road here would be a big mistake.

So off we went to his favorite lake, but only for about 10 minutes, he said, with a soldier-like stern look. It was one of those "get out, look, ah, beautiful, back in and off again" scenes.

Back to the road and then a drive through some beautiful coastal scenes. Ah, but I do miss living near the ocean. Got left on the road to Onuma, across from a *gakko* (school) just getting out for the day.

About 15 little boys in school uniforms spied the funny-looking foreign lady with the pack on her back and came tearing down the hill to get a closer look. At first they all stood around and stared and then started jabbering gibberish at me as if it were English.

I laughed and said in Japanese that I supposed they could speak the language. After a few seconds of gaping at this additional oddity, they caught on and shot a hundred questions at once: "Where did you come from?" "Where are you going?" "What is in the pack?" "What is your name?"

The whole troop of us began flagging down every car that passed. It must have looked hilarious, with dusty rows of houses stretched out behind us and the ocean full out behind that.

They also let me know which cars to ignore. "Not that one. He lets his pigs ride in the truck!" Then I'd say, "No, not that truck, too bumpy. What I want is a sports car!"

They thought that was hilarious, that one should actually *choose* how to ride. Then a little black sports car came along, stopped, I got in, and we all yelled, *"Bai bai!"* The car took off, and the kids ran back up the hill.

The driver was a pro, no less, taking driving very seriously with white gloves and all. Great luck! Being a race car driver would be great fun.

He said the car was only a week old, but despite all its impressively shiny newness, I kept falling asleep anyway and drooling a bit down my chin. Oh, dear.

He hardly talked at all, but was fairly pleasant when he did. He took me off his route all the way to Onuma near the youth hostel. I walked the last kilometer, over the bridge and rather tired. (No real lunch, and only ice cream all day).

Finally arrived at this much-recommended place, nice and very new with all the old customs and good feeling. Very friendly, unserious, and undedicated-spirit types running it. After registering, I walked back to town for cigarettes, eye drops, and after-bath lotion.

June 10, Sunday. Onuma-Hakodate-Ferry-Honshu.

The hostel had the usual evening meeting, with everyone sitting on mats in a circle telling about themselves and their travel in Hokkaido, with me right in there with the best of 'em.

There too, I was a "success." For some I seemed to be the first *gaijin* they had ever met who spoke Japanese. They appreciated, cared, and helped. (Except for the girl on my right who kept touching my pretty brown curls and putting her hand on my knee!)

I sat across from an interesting older couple who had been traveling around the world: he a writer and she his rather mouthy companion.

The hostel *obosans* were a warm, older couple, local farmers. He talked about the area and its history. Why don't they do this at every hostel?

Then others talked, and the meeting ended with music. The *obosan* sang a local folk song, an incredible all-there blend of high mellow sounds. Very beautiful. Then a guitar and song, and good nights.

A Japanese guy and an American guy came in at the end of the meeting. The Japanese guy was a second generation *Nisei* from Hawaii and didn't speak a word of Japanese, and the *gaijin* was from Michigan, had been here in the service, and reads and writes Japanese. I want one of those *Nisei* disguises!

As we talked, I realized how much in need of speaking English I am getting. It's surprising how much it matters. Good to be going back soon.

Up early and to breakfast. Then something nice happened which made me feel how enlivening this trip has been. A small incident but such a different feeling than most of the two rather battering years of living in Kochi and Kyoto.

Walking back to my room after breakfast, I passed the guys' room across the hall. Everyone was at breakfast, except the tough, solid guy, who'd been at the same hostel in Shiraoi with me, was still lying in his bed, propped up on his elbow.

I laughed and said gaily, *"Ohayo gozaimasu! Okite kudasai!"* ("Good morning! Please get up!")

He just put out a lazy arm and with a sleepy smile said, *"Irrasshai!"* ("Come right in!") I laughed and shot back, *"Iyarashii wa, ne!"* ("Nervy, aren't you!") And we both laughed.

Really lovely. Yes, of course, I *am* 27, older than most of the Japanese kids, they probably all know that, but they also see, at least a few of them do, the alive, whole, womanly being I only occasionally am still able to see in myself after being here this long.

It's probably not fair to blame all of that on Japan, but it has been rough in some ways. My boss in Kochi telling me he liked me because I wasn't sexy, meaning what? That he wouldn't want to sleep with me? That, unlike with his other teachers, he knew he couldn't?

Laughed at by hostesses in swanky bars as I stood waiting for the john in my jeans because they thought I was a drunken man who had stumbled in. Drunken restaurant workers sneaking peeks under the curtain at the public bath and shrieking with laughter when they caught sight of my *gaijin* boobs, so everyone in the place was embarrassed and I was near to tears.

Plus, all the incidents women in Japan are constantly aware of: being grabbed in the crotch or swiped across the breasts on crowded subways, followed home late at night, yelled at, laughed at, or pointed at.

Oh, this is such a lovely and aesthetic country. Not so very different from the country I left, only much more harassment as an everyday occurrence.

Later I read an interview with a Japanese woman who said that every Japanese male feels inferior in the presence of a non-Asian woman. Mother of God, I wish they'd told me that earlier!

Just when I am about to leave, I find there are a few likeable men here after all. And I am restored to my own sensuality. Good.

54

To some extent, much of what worked against me in Japan has worked for me in Hokkaido. I needed to be small, sweet, blond, and feminine, their Tuesday Weld image of the foreign female, and then they would've seen I was a woman.

But if I had been all that, I never would have been able to take this trip. Never would have been able to hitch those rides with truck drivers, kept my head well enough, and been so clearly "companion" rather than relegated to the Japanese woman's place. Good!

Sad, in a way, for having wasted all that energy being hurt by people like my boss in Kochi. Well, you won't have to go through this again, will you, m'dear. At least one can hope not. Returning to the US, it'll be the same, only I hope a little less frequent or expected.

Then I left the hostel and was off again, with a big kindly send-off. Headed for Honshu today! Got a ride quickly with a couple of tough nuts.

The passenger was an old man who was a bit much, asking lots of those questions that were none of his business. The driver was young and quiet.

We took off suddenly on another of those dirt roads— and where, pray tell, this time? To one of those horrible summer fairs where horses are tied to cement blocks and raced. I went to them as a kid in Maine and hate them still.

But it was an interesting scene: all the grubby, stony-faced farmers gathered around their workhorses, slapping rumps and placing bets. It turned out that the old guy was the boss of the whole thing. What do you know?

At last we drove out to the road again, and they ended up taking me right to the Honshu ferry. It was then 9:17am and the next ferry was leaving at 9:20am, so I jumped right on. Glad I'd bought a round-trip ticket! And could find it in my backpack.

After several false starts, the ferry slowly pulled out. I stood on the deck and watched the island disappear. A swath of sea spread out behind the ferry, the line of Hokodate smog along the coast left behind.

"Goodbye! Farewell! Thank you! Thank you! I'll be back!"

A Pepsi in one hand, a Seven Stars cigarette in the other, throwing out toasts of love and affection: here's to green fields, schoolboys, cows, and Zen priests. And here's to good young men who know a woman when they see one, and to myself—who has, after all, come through.

Travel is fatal to prejudice, bigotry, and narrow-mindedness, and many of our people need it sorely on these accounts. Broad, wholesome, charitable views of men and things cannot be acquired by vegetating in one little corner of the earth all one's lifetime.
Mark Twain, *The Innocents Abroad*

AFTERWORD
Some of the rest of the story.

The end of June 1973, I flew to San Francisco on a teachers' charter flight for $250. (We knew how to find cheap in those days!) I'd planned to hang around the city for awhile, but found it overwhelming, so I went down to San Bernadino to stay with some friends. I have no idea why I was delaying going back to Maine; giving myself some decompression time, I expect, but I finally did.

At my mother's, nothing had changed, although it's certainly lovely in the summer, with forsythia, rambler roses, daffodils, and Queen Anne's lace. I had a packet of Craig's pictures he'd taken of our *gasshuku* and temple on the mountain, but somehow they disappeared.

Soon, I headed down to Boston to a tribe of long-time friends where I could process my time in Japan and a relationship gone sour. I remember feeling desperate to talk about that time, but quickly realizing the subject hardly interested anyone.

I think many travelers feel the same. It's intense to adapt to another country and then return home, which can feel even more foreign. It's not as strong with a short visit, but a couple years can have an effect.

I found a room in an apartment with two other women in Cambridge and bought a mattress and box spring that I rolled up Inman Square to the apartment.

When Craig had left Japan, I had no idea I'd see him again, but a few weeks later he showed up. He invited me to go back to Japan with him, and I just laughed. I knew I was done, with him and with Japan. His response was to say he'd write a book someday entitled *My Life With Women's Lib.* That was so not my experience, I just laughed some more.

57

Eventually I moved into a three-story apartment building in Somerville filled with eight other women and ended up getting a Master's Degree in Creative Writing in the Feminist Studies Department of Goddard College at a small branch campus across the street.

I worked part-time jobs at American Friends Service Committee in Cambridge, my first exposure to Quakers, and became a kind of personal secretary for a couple of older ladies. One wrote poetry but was fairly deaf and blind; my job was to decipher the keys she'd missed the night before.

The other lady was the mother of a professor at a local college. He went on sabbatical and loaned me his station wagon. I was delighted, but had neglected to tell him I didn't have a license. I quickly corrected things and immediately drove to Toronto to see my friend Sandra, who'd left Japan and was now married and pregnant.

In the course of the next couple years, I met more people connected to the original tribe, including Gary, a quiet guy from Louisiana. After a year and a half courtship, we were married in 1976. His final Northeastern University law school co-op job was at Florida Rural Legal Services (FRLS) in Delray Beach, Florida, so off we went. (For some reason, I thought Delray was on the Panhandle. Life before GPS!)

We'd bought a car out of a snowdrift in Allston for $300, filled it with wedding presents and our cat Fido, and headed south. We discovered fairly soon the transmission was seriously impaired and switched it for a VW Rabbit once we hit Florida. No AC, but in those early days, we thought it didn't matter. We didn't know how AC-dependent we'd become. A Florida thing.

The state was a shock. It was February, and amazingly, there'd just been snow in Palm Beach County. But from Jacksonville on, it felt like the hottest place I'd ever been. We came for a three-month co-op job, extended to six, then Gary passed the Florida bar, FRLS hired him, and we realized we had settled in.

It's been 46 years now. Gulp. We rented for a couple years, had a son, then a daughter, bought a small house, and then sold it for a house in Wellington, western Palm Beach County, where the schools were good. And then, of course, the kids grew up and moved away.

I joined a Quaker Meeting and a member who taught at a local college asked why I wasn't teaching. Goddard was hippie, sure, but accredited. I picked up a couple of classes to teach, but also got a second master's in literature to look more legitimate.

I ended up teaching at several local colleges, mostly as an adjunct, for the next 30 years. (Let me add: adjunct positions are exploitative, allow colleges to avoid paying benefits, and are not a stable source of income, but can be helpful for people with day jobs and parents who want time at home with kids.)

The property development of Florida has been a constant. Surprisingly a third of Palm Beach Country is farmland, sugar cane and vegetables. The county goes from Palm Beach opulence to Belle Glade poverty.

We've also gotten used to the yearly influx of "snowbirds" who come down to avoid northern winters. The traffic by Thanksgiving is horrendous.

The last few years, Palm Beach County has had fewer hurricanes, but the whole state's an annual target from June 1st to November 30th. Insurance companies are leaving in droves, which should bring some attention to the climate crisis. Not much else seems to be working.

I retired early and decided to prioritize the writing I'd been doing all my life. For a couple years, I uploaded my books to Amazon Kindle as ebooks.

Later, I wrote *The Little Quaker Book of Weight Loss* and a friend offered to publish it for our Quaker conference that was coming up. At the last minute, she couldn't, but I'd gotten the bug.

I paid a local newspaper editor $100 to do the layout, printed out a draft, took it to Office Depot, and made 20 copies. I folded and collated the pages at the kitchen table, went back to Office Depot to use the long stapler, and sold all the copies at the conference. My publishing career was launched!

I've now published 14 books. I am among the millions of writers around the world who utilize self-publishing. I tried for years in my twenties to get the attention of an agent or publisher and nothing much happened. Vanity presses were highly disparaged in the past and expensive, but now self-publishing is possible and inexpensive. I've seen some poor quality; everyone has. We writers always think we know best and our work doesn't need proofreading.

But I'm dogged about editing and am fortunate to have friends as first readers who always find the one error I've missed in 15 edits.

This is obviously not a rich and famous writer story, so why do I keep doing it? Well, on some level, it comes down to not being able to *not* do it. Writing feels like a spiritual exercise in some way and gives purpose as my life winds down into the later years.

I share my books with friends, sell some to benefit our Quaker conference, and find my books lead quite a few people to form discussion groups or think further about burning issues in our world.

The other day a new friend downloaded *Rising Still, Breaking Through the Sadness of Women,* which I wrote in 2006, about what to do after the kids leave, and she said she could relate. You never know where the words will go. It seems I wrote that for her.

David Bowie said, "Aging is an extraordinary process whereby you become the person you always should have been." Some of the early conditioning sloughs off, we figure out how to keep ourselves going, and we learn to avoid, or deal better with, guilt, anger, depression, and anxiety.

We begin to value who we are, consider our pasts with compassion, and cultivate some gratitude for still being here and the gifts that surround us.

Out of this "taking stock" has come the impetus to publish the *Hokkaido Journal*. Here's primary source material for who I was fifty years ago. It's been fun to work on, consider what it meant, and what it means now.

But also, no need to go over the top with "what it all means." It was. I was. And still am—a person who loves adventure, though milder ones these days, loves hearing a story I've never heard before, and can't wait for the next meal. (Just not raw eggs!)

I'll end by repeating my earlier encouragement to all those "of a certain age." Take a dip in your past. Look at a time in your life when you were becoming who you are now. Dare to think about what was going on, who you loved, and who you left behind. It's a kind of accounting: what we have managed to do with what Mary Oliver has called our "wild and precious life."

Perhaps, we'll discover we've done a fair job of making a life, being a human being, and fulfilling a kind of destiny that maybe becomes clearer as we approach the end. And from there, who knows?

To travel is to live.
Hans Christian Andersen

Life is either a daring adventure or nothing at all.
Helen Keller

I am not the same having seen the moon shine on the other side of the world.
Mary Anne Radmacher

ACKNOWLEDGEMENTS

Heartfelt thanks to everyone who participated in bringing *Hokkaido Journal* into print: Zen priests, over-extended travelers, a long-ago boyfriend, hostel parents, and protection from somewhere that let me live the experience and live this long to tell the tale. My gratitude to first readers Linda Karon in Wellington, FL, Sandra Sewell, on Tamborine Mountain in Australia, and Jean Scoon in Wisconsin. You have all made this a better book. And special thanks to Thecla Geraghty in London, UK, for her skillful rendition of a map of the meandering trek. Any geographical confusion is all mine. Big thanks to husband Gary for taking on the publisher role. Miraculously, we're still married. Thanks to friends who've put up with the conversations and given encouragement for digging up the past. And special thanks to the one person out there—probably a woman—who might say, "You wrote this for me."

AUTHOR PAGE

Ellie Caldwell continues to live in South Florida, married to Gary for 47 years, with two aloof cats, a jungly backyard, and too many books. With grandchildren in Atlanta now, a move may be in the future, but not yet. She's still saying "the 70s rock" though fears for the soul of our nation. Y'all get out and vote!

Made in the USA
Columbia, SC
13 June 2024

36526517R10039